DRAGONS OF MOON TAIL ISLAND

Written by Jo Cotterill
Illustrated by Lisa Hunt

OXFORD
UNIVERSITY PRESS

Meet the characters ...

One quiet afternoon, Nadia was lying on the sofa. Dad was in the shop looking after customers. Omar was drawing a picture of a dragon.

'I miss Ember,' sighed Nadia.

'Me too,' said Omar.

Suddenly, there was a tap on the window. 'Ember!' cried Nadia.

The children went out into the yard.

'Do you want to come flying?' asked Ember.

'Yes, please!' cheered Omar.

The children climbed onto her back. Ember took off.

Down below, Mrs McKinley was out for a walk. Poly was on her shoulder. The parrot squawked when she saw Ember.

Is the lamppost **taller than** or **shorter than** the tree next to the path?

Ember soared over the countryside. Soon they landed in a field near some woods.

'I have a surprise for you,' sang Ember, as the children slid from her back. She turned to the woods. 'Nimbus!' she called. 'You can come out now!'

Another dragon appeared from behind a large bush. He had light blue scales and large wings. The children gasped.

'Nimbus is a cloud dragon,' said Ember. 'He's my best friend on Moon Tail Island.'

'Pleased to meet you,' said Nimbus.

Look at Nimbus's wings. Do you think they are **longer than** or **shorter than** Ember's wings?

‘Ember told me you like flying,’ Nimbus said.

‘Nimbus is the best flyer I know,’ added Ember. ‘How would you like to learn some new moves?’

‘That would be amazing!’ said Nadia.

Omar climbed onto Nimbus. Nadia climbed onto Ember.

'We are going to practise a running take off first,' said Ember. 'You both need to hold on tight!'

'It might get bumpy,' said Nimbus, chuckling.

Nadia is on Ember and together they are 3 **metres** tall. Which is taller, 3 **metres** or 3 **centimetres**?

'One, two, three, go!' called Ember.

The two dragons raced across the field. Their feet thudded on the grass.

Nimbus ran 40 **metres**. Ember ran 30 **metres**. Who ran the greater distance?

‘Very good,’ Nimbus said. ‘You both held on very tight.’

‘Now let’s race back,’ said Ember. ‘One, two, three, go!’

The dragons sped off the way they had come.

Nimbus ran 40 **metres**. Ember ran 50 **metres**. Who ran the greater distance?

The children and dragons didn't notice that Poly was watching them. 'Dragon!' she squawked. She looked again. '*Dragons!*' she squawked. She began to race after them.

However, parrots are much **shorter than** dragons. It was difficult for Poly to run in the grass.

First, Poly ran 86**cm**. Then she ran 60**cm**. Which is the greater distance?

Meanwhile, the dragons were practising another move. 'Now we're going to run, take off, and fly straight up,' said Nimbus. 'We'll go as high as that tree. Let's go!'

Nadia gasped as Ember took off …

The dragons flew straight up to the top of the tree then straight back down.

'That was fun,' Nadia said, once they had landed.

'Let's try the next tree,' Ember said. 'It's **taller than** this one.'

They zoomed to the top of another tree.

‘Now,’ Nimbus said. ‘We’ll do some difficult moves.’

The dragons looped and swooped in the air.

Poly was still trying to catch up with the dragons.

She flew up to the top of a bench. Then she looked for something **taller than** it. She flew up to the top of a fence, then a tree.

The bench is 1 **metre** tall. The fence is 2 **metres** tall. The tree is 6 **metres** tall. What is **taller than** the fence? What is **shorter than** the tree?

Soon Poly felt dizzy. She zigzagged through the air, squawking.

Nadia spotted her. 'Look!' she said. 'It's Poly!'

Suddenly, Poly fell and crashed into some soft leaves.

The dragons landed and the children went running over to the parrot.
'Poly, are you all right?' asked Nadia.

Poly's feathers were ruffled, but she wasn't hurt.

Then Mrs McKinley arrived. 'There you are, Poly!' she said. She turned to the children. 'Thank you for finding her.'

'Dragons!' squawked Poly.

'Dragons indeed!' laughed Mrs McKinley. 'Let's go home, Poly.'

The dragons came out from where they'd been hiding.

'Poor Poly,' said Ember.

'Luckily your flying skills are much better than Poly's!' said Nadia.

‘Today’s practice wasn’t just for fun,’ said Ember. ‘Nimbus and I are going to take you to Moon Tail Island!’

Nadia and Omar gasped.

‘Ember is going to have a party soon,’ Nimbus explained.

‘I want you both to come,’ said Ember.

Nadia and Omar looked at each other with huge grins.

'Are you ready for our biggest adventure yet?' asked Ember.

'Yes!' they cheered.

'I've always wondered what Moon Tail Island is like,' said Nadia.

'Well,' chuckled Ember, 'very soon you'll find out!'

Spot the difference

Can you spot the 6 differences in the pictures?
Use these words to help describe what you find.

length, height, taller than, longer than, shorter than, greater than, less than

Answers

p5. taller than; p7. longer than; p9. 3 metres; p10. Nimbus; p11. Ember; p13. 86 cm; p17. The tree is taller than the fence; The bench and fence are shorter than the tree; p24. In the bottom picture, Mrs McKinley's boots are shorter, the map under her arm is longer, the fence is taller and shorter in length, Nimbus's tail is shorter, and the height of the bush is shorter than in the top picture.